BASIC SKILLS

HAL LEONARD STUDENT PIANO

Rhythm With The Blues

A Comprehensive Rhythm Program for Musicians

Volume 3

TABLE OF CONTENTS

ISBN 978-0-6340-8806-3

HAL•LEONARD®
CORPORATION

7777 W. BLUEMOUND RD. P.O. BOX 13819 MILWAUKEE, WI 53213

Visit Hal Leonard Online at
www.halleonard.com

A Note to Students

Welcome to *Rhythm Without the Blues* – Volume Three. This unique program will take you from the very basics of rhythm to an advanced level of comprehension and performance ability. The materials in your workbook, combined with practice exercises and demonstrations on the CD, work together to bring a clear understanding of the basics of rhythm. The demonstrations, exercises, and dictations will give you the necessary practice so that you will be equipped to understand and perform a vast array of rhythmic patterns.

You will find this series easy to use. This series will require a metronome and a CD player.

Each chapter is divided into smaller sections. This allows you to work at one section for a short period of time. Working in small sections is more valuable than trying to cover large amounts of material. Learning this way lays a good foundation as you continue to build your skills.

All exercises and dictations may be used repeatedly for additional practice or review. For written exercises, you may either erase your answers or use a separate sheet of paper.

YOUR CD:

- You may access tracks on your CD by moving from smaller numbers up or from larger numbers down. Simply press the track buttons to find the desired track number.

▶▶❘ • This button will move forward through the CD.

❘◀◀ • This button will move backward through the CD.

- The dictations and exercises are played once. Repeat tracks as many times as necessary to complete each exercise.

YOUR WORKBOOK:

METRONOME: This program requires the use of a metronome, so let's discuss this first.

In 1816, a man by the name of Maelzel manufactured a mechanical device which sounded an adjustable number of beats per minute. Whenever a composer wants the speed or tempo of their piece to be fixed at a certain number of beats per minute—let's say 60, for example—they will write "M.M." plus the symbol for a note equals 60, just as you see in the box below. The "M.M." stands for Maelzel's Metronome. The number 60 simply indicates that the metronome will beat 60 times per minute. In your workbook, the symbol for the metronome is shown as a bell, as seen below.

Metronome speed is indicated like this:

🔔 **M.M. ♩ = 60**

This is how it will be shown throughout this series.

Take some time to consult the manual for your metronome and familiarize yourself with its operation and how it sounds at different settings.

The metronome sound is given to help you establish a standard by which to judge the rhythmic pattern. Each bell represents one pulse or beat of the metronome.

On the CD, you will hear the metronome give a count-off before every exercise or dictation. This will prepare you for the beginning of the exercise or dictation.

NOTATION

You will notice that only the stems of the notes are being used, as indicated below:

Noteheads will only be shown when they are needed to indicate the time value of the rhythm. This will become clear as you progress through the book.

HEADINGS

All of the chapters are set up in the same way. Headings appear on the left-hand side of the page, which introduce a series of tasks designed to familiarize you with various rhythmic patterns.

NEW ELEMENT

Under this heading, you will see a large subdivided table. The first section of the table, **Rhythm**, shows what the rhythm symbol looks like. The second section, **Term**, gives the technical name. The third section, **Value**, tells how many beats that rhythm is worth. In the last section, **Rhythm Name**, a spoken syllable is assigned to that rhythm. See **NEW ELEMENT** p. 9 for an example.

LISTENING

Under this heading, you will be given an opportunity to listen to what the rhythm sounds like on the CD. In the example, you will hear two sounds: (1) the metronome and (2) an instrument sounding the rhythmic pattern on a single pitch.

The example will be demonstrated first. You will then have a chance to practice tapping the example. To tap rhythms, strike the tips of your fingers on the edge of a table, palm facing down. Following this, a musical example containing the new element will usually be heard. See **LISTENING** p. 9 for an example.

TAPPING

Material under this heading presents you with an opportunity to practice the new element without the CD.

You will use your metronome to help keep a steady beat. The metronome marking is indicated beside the heading. Set your metronome to the tempo shown.

You will want to learn to feel the basic beat by tapping it yourself. Begin tapping an even beat, equivalent to the metronome, with the hand opposite the one with which you will be tapping the rhythmic patterns. If you are right-handed, you will probably be tapping the rhythms with your right hand and the metronome beat with your left hand. When you have established a steady beat with one hand, begin tapping the rhythmic patterns with the other hand. At first it might feel like rubbing your head and patting your stomach at the same time, but as you persevere, it will become more and more natural for you. See **TAPPING** p. 10 for an example.

MATCHING

Under this heading, you will see a series of boxes containing rhythmic patterns. Here you will match the patterns you hear on the CD, in correct sequence, by indicating the corresponding letters in the spaces provided. Note that most of the rhythms played on the CD consist of a combination of more than one of the boxes given. See **MATCHING** p. 11 for an example.

DICTATION

The next heading contains a series of exercises in which you will write down the rhythmic patterns that you hear.

Only the stems of rhythmic patterns will be used. This is a form of rhythmic shorthand which will help as you write the dictations. Develop your own shorthand in dictations. For example, if you need to write a series of notes that are joined at the top, simply write the basic outline and fill in the rest later. This will become easier as you progress.

On the CD, you will hear each dictation once. Repeat the tracks as often as necessary to complete each exercise.

- First, listen and tap along with the metronome. Listen closely for the rhythmic pattern associated with each beat.

- Speak the rhythm name associated with each pattern, for example, *ti-ti* or *ta*. You may want to do this more than once.

- Next, begin to fill in the patterns under the metronome symbols using the rhythmic shorthand. Write in as many patterns as you can remember each time.

See **DICTATION** p. 12 for an example.

INTEGRATION

Exercises under this heading introduce a melodic component, added to help develop well-rounded listening skills. It is important to begin to hear not only rhythmic patterns, but melodic movement as well. See **INTEGRATION** p. 13 for an example.

Remember, with the exercises and dictations, it is accuracy that counts. Speed will come later.

You and your teacher may want to chart your progress. Try keeping a log showing the number of times you had to listen to the exercises before completing them and how accurately you were able to tap exercises the first time.

We recommend that you use the companion series:

Ear Without Fear

Ear Without Fear is a comprehensive ear-training program. Using these two series together will help you to successfully master the dictations and exercises in Levels 3 and 4.

A Note to Teachers

Rhythm Without the Blues is an innovative program aimed at building a clear understanding of rhythm and the ability to perform it accurately.

Rhythm is a complex task that is mathematical in structure. It is distinct from ear training, which has a melodic component and employs different neurological pathways, yet both elements are invariably placed together in music training. The result is often frustration and a sense of failure. Ultimately, these elements will be combined. Levels 3 and 4 provide exercises that integrate rhythmic and melodic components.

We have carefully chosen and organized the materials in this book to make the learning process as accessible to students as possible. The Workbook and the CD are integrated to provide several learning approaches: AURAL, VISUAL, and PRACTICAL. Together, they present a comprehensive, step-by-step learning program for which the student can assume primary responsibility.

The following concepts will be covered in Volume 3:

- Note and rest recognition
- Time signatures $\frac{2}{2}$ and ¢
- Note and rest groupings in the time signatures
- Demonstrations, exercises, and dictations covering these areas

Stems will be used to indicate time values. Noteheads are not used unless the notehead indicates the value of that rhythm. This enables the student to focus solely on the rhythmic elements. Rhythm names will be used to facilitate recognition of rhythmic elements. The rhythm names used have been adapted from those developed and advanced by Emile-Joseph Chevé, John Curwen, Zoltán Kodály, and Pierre Perron.

Here is why teachers are finding this series an invaluable aid in the studio and classroom:

- It provides a prepared curriculum.
- Students can work independently with well-formatted, easily understood materials.
- Chapters are easily subdivided for appropriately sized weekly assignments.
- Exercises and dictations are readily available for weekly testing and instruction.
- Lesson time is maximized for instrument instruction, while ensuring the student is honing musicianship skills.

Students often find the development of essential rhythmic and aural skills less exciting than learning an instrument, so a reward system may be helpful. Consider implementing one, using some of the following suggestions:

- Encourage students to keep a log, outlining the number of sections and exercises completed over the week. They may also want to keep track of how long it takes to complete each exercise. Students' confidence will grow as they begin to see an increase in proficiency and speed.

- Award incentive points for successful completion of sections and increased proficiency. Give prizes and awards based on accumulated points.

It is recommended that students also use the companion series:

Ear Without Fear

Ear Without Fear is a comprehensive ear-training program that works in tandem with *Rhythm Without the Blues*. Using them together will greatly enhance the ability of the student to successfully master the dictations and exercises contained in each series.

CHAPTER 1

NEW ELEMENT

Rhythm	Term	Value	Rhythm Name
$\overset{3}{\sqcap}$	triplet	one beat	tri - o - la

Our new rhythm element is in simple time.

This element introduces us to an exception in musical mathematics. The *tri-o-la* is made up of three eighth notes joined at the top by a beam. Normally this would equal one and one half beats. However, the three notes in a TRIPLET are tapped out evenly in the space of one beat.

The little 3 over the middle stem of the grouping is the indication to tap this in a different way. The triplet has a combined value of one quarter note.

LISTENING

 PLAY CD TRACK 1

Example A

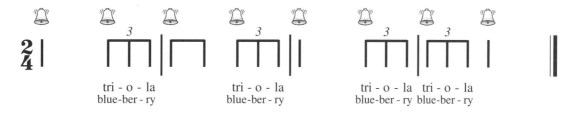

In traditional counting, it is common practice to use three syllable words or phrases,
such as blueberry, strawberry, or cup-of-tea.
For our purposes, we have chosen to use the word blueberry.

A theme in the second movement of Tchaikovsky's Symphony No. 6 uses the triplet to beautiful effect.

TAPPING

For each of the following exercises, tap the rhythm pattern with one hand and the basic beat with the opposite hand. By now you will have the skill to maintain a steady beat. Therefore, it will not always be necessary for you to use your metronome.

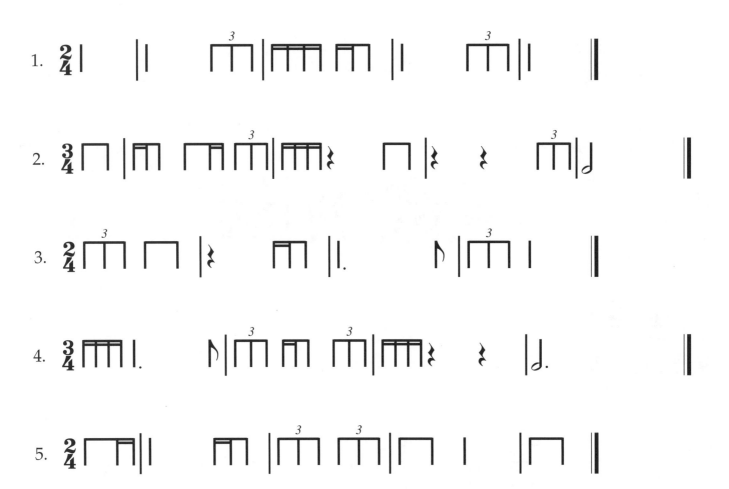

*The metronome beat will no longer be heard except for the initial strikes
to establish the start of each exercise.
It will be important for you to continue to tap the basic beat as the exercise plays.*

MATCHING

Using the rhythm boxes below, find the rhythms that match the exercises on CD tracks 3–4. Each exercise consists of more than one rhythm box and is played once on the CD. Note that when there is a pick-up measure, the metronome sound the missing beat(s) before the exercise begins. Write your answers in the spaces provided. Answers are on page 44.

 PLAY CD TRACK 3

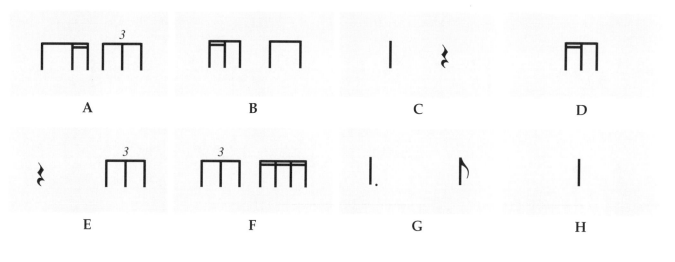

1. _____ 2. _____ 3. _____ 4. _____

 PLAY CD TRACK 4

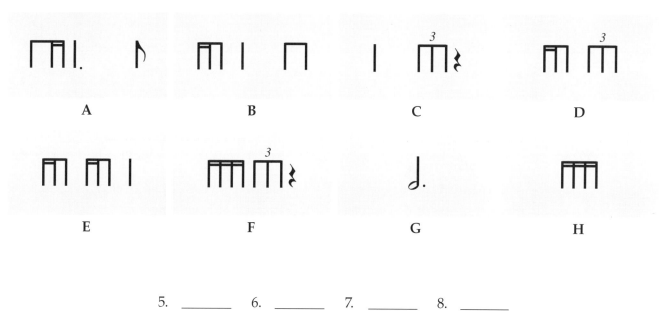

5. _____ 6. _____ 7. _____ 8. _____

From this chapter on, metronome symbols will no longer be given for dictations.

DICTATION

Play the tracks one at a time. Write the rhythm pattern that you hear. Answers are on page 44.

PLAY CD TRACKS 5–8

1. $\frac{3}{4}$ | | | | |

2. $\frac{2}{4}$ | | | | |

3. $\frac{3}{4}$ | | | |

4. $\frac{2}{4}$ | | | | |

Until now, we have been writing rhythmic dictations without a melody. We will now begin a section in each chapter called INTEGRATION in which rhythmic and melodic elements are combined.

> We recommend the companion series *Ear Without Fear!*, a comprehensive ear-training program that works in tandem with *Rhythm Without the Blues*. Using them together will greatly enhance the ability of the student to successfully master the dictations and exercises contained in each series.

The CD will give you a dictation in melodic form. First, write the rhythms you hear above the staff. Then listen for the sol-fa and write in the melody. Lastly, complete the notes you have entered on the staff with the correct stems.

Study the steps below.

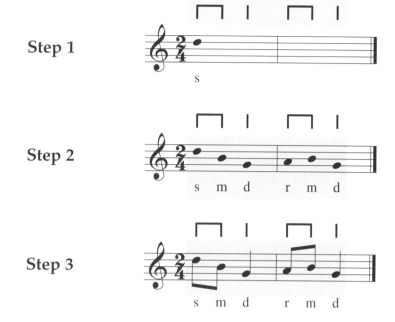

Step 1

Step 2

Step 3

INTEGRATION

Play the tracks one at a time. Write the melody that you hear. The starting pitch is given. First, write the rhythm pattern in the space above the staff and then draw the corresponding pitches on the staff. Finally, add stems to the noteheads to complete the dictation. Answers are on page 44.

 PLAY CD TRACKS 9–10

1.

d

2.

m

Introduction of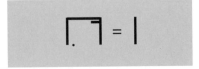

NEW ELEMENT

Rhythm	Term	Value	Rhythm Name
⌐⌐	dotted eighth, one sixteenth	one beat	tim-ka

$$ \text{⌐⌐} = | $$

Once again we will be considering a new element in simple time.

We will now look at the dotted eighth followed by a sixteenth. Remember, the dot after a note increases that note's value by one half. In this case, the dot has the same time value as a sixteenth note. This pattern is tapped within the space of one beat, but the dotted eighth is sustained slightly, giving it a "long-short" feeling. Study the note value relationships shown at the right.

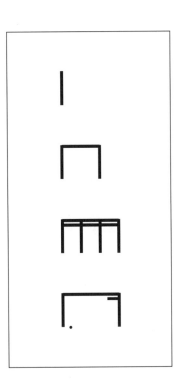

LISTENING

PLAY CD TRACK 11

Example A

PLAY CD TRACK 12

This aria from *The Marriage of Figaro* by Mozart shows us what a *tim-ka* sounds like.

TAPPING

For each of the following exercises, tap the rhythm pattern with one hand and the basic beat with the opposite hand.

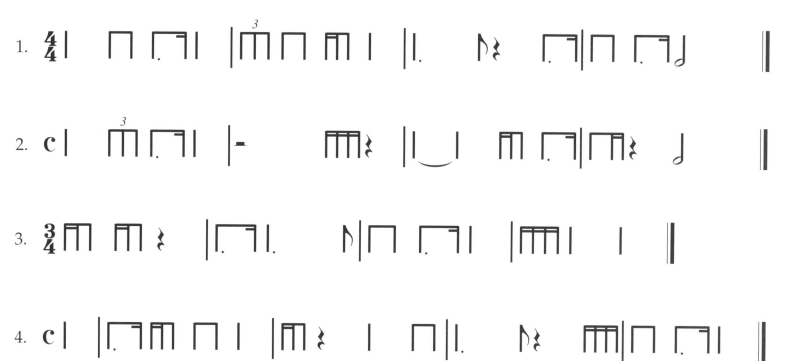

MATCHING

Match the rhythm boxes shown below with the corresponding exercises on the CD. Mark your answers in the spaces provided. Each exercise consists of more than one rhythm box and is played once on the CD. Answers are on page 44.

 PLAY CD TRACK 13

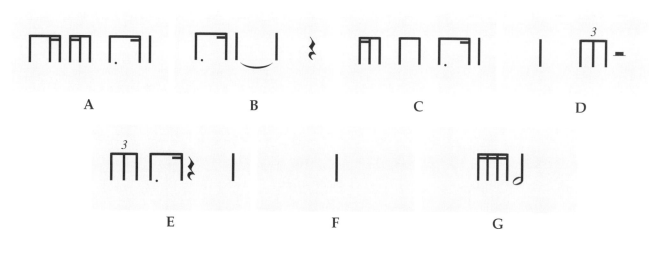

PLAY CD TRACK 14

A	B	C	D
E	F	G	H

1. _____ 2. _____ 3. _____ 4. _____

DICTATION

Play the tracks one at a time. Write the rhythm pattern that you hear. Answers are one page 44.

PLAY CD TRACKS 15–18

1. **C**

2. **3/4**

3. **4/4**

4. **3/4**

INTEGRATION

Play the tracks one at a time. Write the melody that you hear. The starting pitch is given. First, write the rhythm pattern in the space above the staff and then draw the corresponding pitches on the staff. Finally, add stems to the noteheads to complete the dictation. Answers are on page 44.

 PLAY CD TRACKS 19–20

1.

d

2.

s

CHAPTER 3

Introduction of ♫.

NEW ELEMENT

Rhythm	Term	Value	Rhythm Name
♫.	one sixteenth, dotted eighth	one beat	ti-kam

♫. = ♩   ♫. = ♫

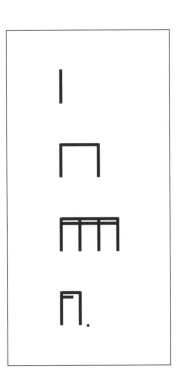

This pattern is the reverse of *tim-ka*. It is made up of a sixteenth and a dotted eighth. This pattern is also tapped within the space of one beat with the sixteenth tapped quickly and the dotted eighth sustained slightly, giving it a "short-long" feeling. Study the note value relationships shown at the right.

LISTENING

PLAY CD TRACK 21

Example A

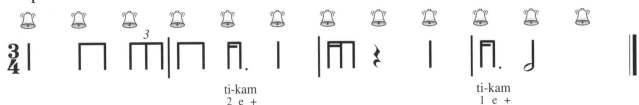

ti-kam
2 e +

ti-kam
1 e +

PLAY CD TRACK 22

The Italian aria *Se tu m'ami* by Parisotti demonstrates this rhythm pattern.

ti-kam   tikam

TAPPING

For each of the following exercises, tap the rhythm pattern with one hand and the basic beat with the opposite hand.

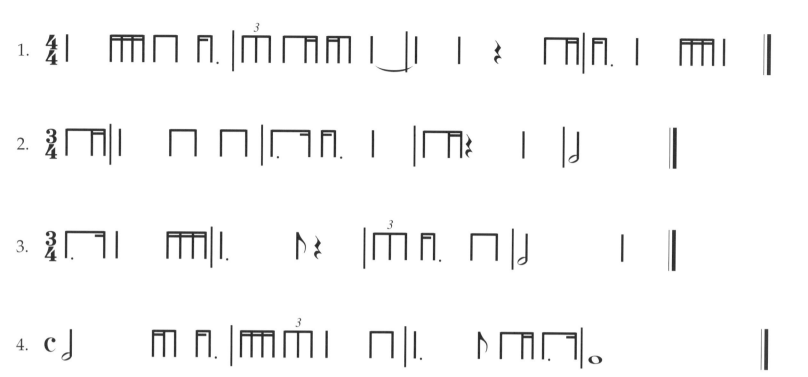

MATCHING

Match the rhythm boxes shown below with the corresponding exercises on the CD. Mark your answers in the spaces provided. Each exercise consists of more than one rhythm box and is played once on the CD. Answers are on page 45.

 PLAY CD TRACK 23

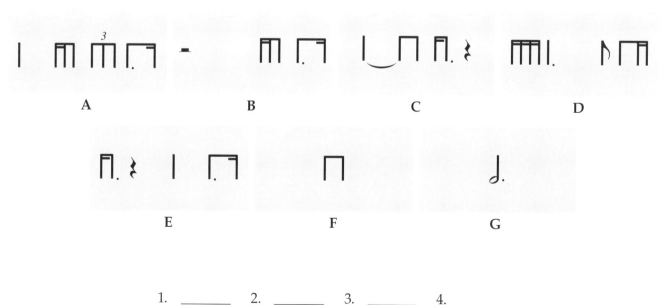

A	B	C	D

E	F	G	H

5. _____   6. _____   7. _____   8. _____

DICTATION

Play the tracks one at a time. Write the rhythm pattern that you hear. Answers are on page 45.

 PLAY CD TRACK 25–28

1. $\frac{4}{4}$

2. $\frac{3}{4}$

3. $\mathbf{C}$

4. $\frac{3}{4}$

INTEGRATION

Play the tracks one at a time. Write the melody that you hear. The starting pitch is given. First, write the rhythm pattern in the space above the staff and then draw the corresponding pitches on the staff. Finally, add stems to the noteheads to complete the dictation. Answers are on page 45.

PLAY CD TRACK 29–30

CHAPTER 4

Introduction of ♪ and 7

Our next new elements have the same value as half a quarter-note beat. The *ti* symbol is made up of a single stem, with a flag or tail on the right side. The single eighth is worth half a quarter note. The eighth rest is also worth half a quarter beat.

NEW ELEMENT

Rhythm	Term	Value	Rhythm Name
♪	eighth	half beat	ti

Rhythm	Term	Value	Rhythm Name
7	eighth rest	half beat	sh

LISTENING

PLAY CD TRACK 31

Example A

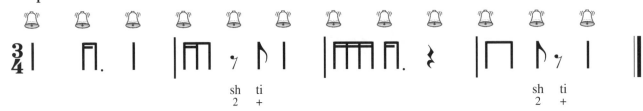

TAPPING

For each of the following exercises, tap the rhythm pattern with one hand and the basic beat with the opposite hand.

1.

2.

3.

4.

MATCHING

Match the rhythm boxes shown below with the corresponding exercises on the CD. Mark your answers in the spaces provided. Each exercise consists of more than one rhythm box and is played once on the CD. Answers are on page 45.

 PLAY CD TRACK 32

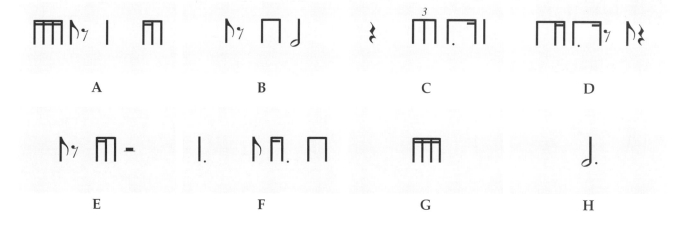

    A   B   C   D

    E   F   G   H

1. _____ 2. _____ 3. _____ 4. _____

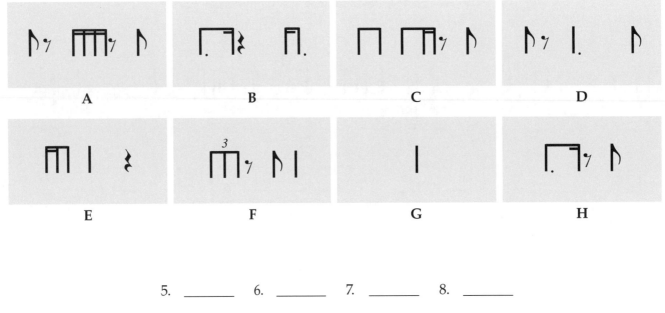

5. _____ 6. _____ 7. _____ 8. _____

1. To draw an eighth rest, begin by drawing a dot

2. Then without lifting your pencil add a "7"

Using these examples as a guide, practise drawing this symbol in the space below.

DICTATION

Play the tracks one at a time. Write the rhythm pattern that you hear. Answers are on page 45.

 PLAY CD TRACKS 34–37

1. $\mathbf{\frac{3}{4}}$

2. $\mathbf{\frac{3}{4}}$

3. $\frac{4}{4}$ | | | ‖

4. 𝐂 | | | ‖

 INTEGRATION

Play the tracks one at a time. Write the melody that you hear.
Answers are on page 45.

PLAY CD TRACKS 38–39

1.
d

2.
s

CHAPTER 5

Introduction of $\frac{2}{2}$ and ¢ time signatures

We now have a new simple time signature.

In example A below, the top number 2 in the time signature indicates two beats per measure, and the bottom number 2 represents a half note, which means that there will be the equivalent of two half beats in every bar. A measure of $\frac{2}{2}$ time resembles a measure in $\frac{4}{4}$ or common time. However, instead of feeling the pulse of four quarter notes per bar, in $\frac{2}{2}$ time we feel the pulse of two half notes per bar. Because of this, it is also known as CUT TIME, indicated with the symbol ¢.

Another way to think of it is like this: $\frac{2}{\downarrow}$

LISTENING

 PLAY CD TRACK 40

Example A

As in $\frac{2}{4}$, $\frac{3}{4}$, and $\frac{4}{4}$ time, there is a natural accent on the first beat of each bar.
The beat emphasis in $\frac{2}{2}$ or cut time is as follows: Strong, weak.

 PLAY CD TRACK 41

The overture to Mozart's opera *The Marriage of Figaro* is in cut time. Listen for the two main beats in each bar.

TAPPING

For each of the following exercises, tap the rhythm pattern with one hand and the basic beat with the opposite hand.

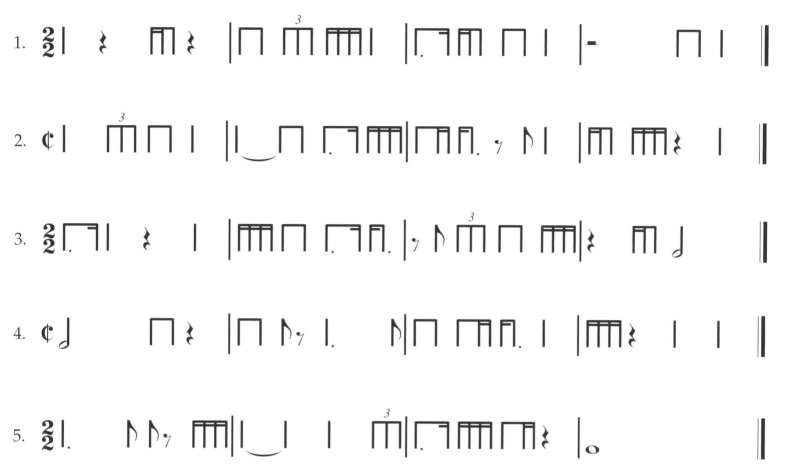

MATCHING

Match the rhythm boxes shown below with the corresponding exercises on the CD. Mark your answers in the spaces provided. Each exercise consists of more than one rhythm box and is played once on the CD. Answers are on page 46.

 PLAY CD TRACK 42

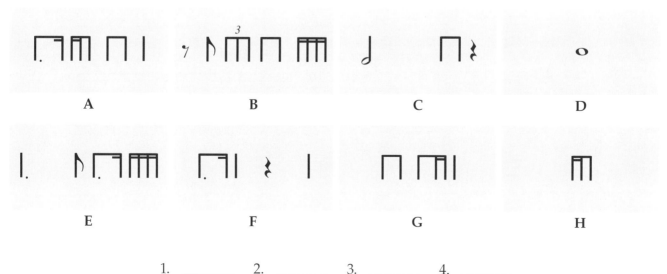

1. _____   2. _____   3. _____   4. _____

DICTATION

Play the tracks one at a time. Write the rhythm pattern that you hear.
Answers are on page 46.

 PLAY CD TRACKS 43–46

1. ¢

2. 𝄵 (2/2)

3. ¢

4. 𝄵 (2/2)

INTEGRATION

Play the tracks one at a time. Write the melody that you hear.
Answers are on page 46.

 PLAY CD TRACKS 47–48

1. 𝄢 ♭ 2/2
   d

2. 𝄞 ♯ ¢
   s

CHAPTER 6

Introduction of ♪ ⌐.

NEW ELEMENT

Rhythm	Term	Value	Rhythm Name
♪ ⌐.	one eighth, dotted quarter	two beats	ti-tam

Ti-tam is the reverse of *tam-ti*. An eighth and a dotted quarter combine to equal two beats. When tapped, this rhythm will feel like "short-long."

$$♪⌐. = ⊓⊓ \qquad ♪⌐. = |\ \ |$$

LISTENING

PLAY CD TRACK 49

Example A

PLAY CD TRACK 50

Listen to the *ti-tam* in "He's Got the Whole World in His Hand."

TAPPING

For each of the following exercises, tap the rhythm pattern with one hand and the basic beat with the opposite hand.

1.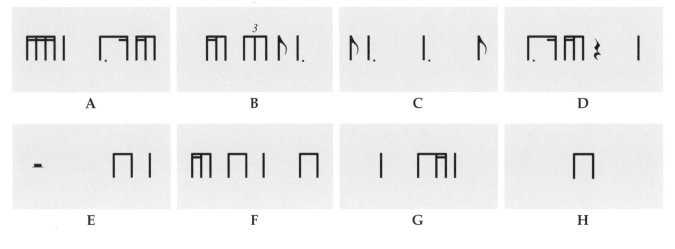

2.

3.

4.

5.

MATCHING

Match the rhythm boxes shown below with the corresponding exercises on the CD. Mark your answers in the spaces provided. Each exercise consists of more than one rhythm box and is played once on the CD. Answers are on page 46.

 PLAY CD TRACK 51

A

B

C

D

E

F

G

H

1. _____   2. _____   3. _____   4. _____

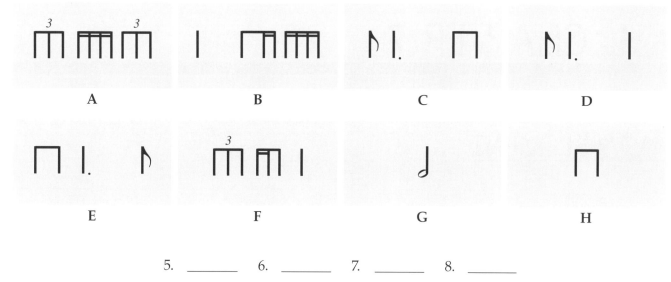

A   B   C   D

E   F   G   H

5. _____ 6. _____ 7. _____ 8. _____

DICTATION

Play the tracks one at a time. Write the rhythm pattern that you hear. Answers are on page 46.

 PLAY CD TRACKS 53–56

INTEGRATION

Play the tracks one at a time. Write the melody that you hear. Answers are on page 46.

PLAY CD TRACKS 57–58

CHAPTER 7

Introduction of ♪ | ♪

NEW ELEMENT

Rhythm	Term	Value	Rhythm Name
♪ | ♪	one eighth, one quarter, one eighth	two beats	syn-co-pa

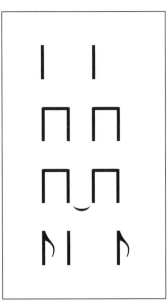

♪ | ♪ = ⊓ ⊓   ♪ | ♪ = | |

The *syn-co-pa* symbol is made up of an eighth note, followed by a quarter note, followed by an eighth note. These combine to equal two beats. It is called a syncopated rhythm because the beat emphasis is in an unexpected place. Study the note value relationships shown at the right.

LISTENING

 PLAY CD TRACK 59

Example A

syn-co - pa
1 + 2 +

syn-co - pa
1 + 2 +

 PLAY CD TRACK 60

The well-known "Allegro" from Vivaldi's *The Four Seasons* clearly demonstrates the *syn-co-pa*.

syn-co - pa   syn-co - pa   syn-co - pa

This rhythm pattern needs to be practiced slowly so that the hand tapping the rhythm can coordinate with the hand tapping the basic beat. Notice that both hands begin together and then tap independently to complete the pattern.

TAPPING

For each of the following exercises, tap the rhythm pattern with one hand and the basic beat with the opposite hand.

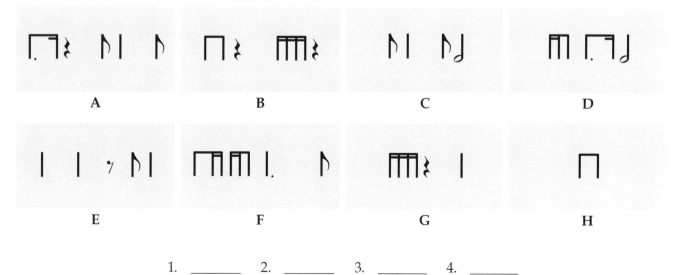

MATCHING

Match the rhythm boxes shown below with the corresponding exercises on the CD. Mark your answers in the spaces provided. Each exercise consists of more than one rhythm box and is played once on the CD. Answers are on **page 47**.

 PLAY CD TRACK 61

1. _____ 2. _____ 3. _____ 4. _____

A	B	C	D
E	F	G	H

5. _____ 6. _____ 7. _____ 8. _____

DICTATION

Play the tracks one at a time. Write the rhythm pattern that you hear. Answers are on page 47.

1. $\frac{4}{4}$ | | | |

2. $\frac{3}{4}$ | | | ‖

3. ¢ | | | |

4. $\frac{3}{4}$ | | | | ‖

INTEGRATION

Play the tracks one at a time. Write the melody that you hear. Answers are on page 47.

Answers are on page 47.

PLAY CD TRACKS 67–68

1. (treble clef, one sharp, common time)

    d

2. (bass clef, 6/8 time)

    m

CHAPTER 8

Introduction of

NEW ELEMENT

Rhythm	Term	Value	Rhythm Name
	one sixteenth, one eighth, one sixteenth	one beat	syn-co-pa

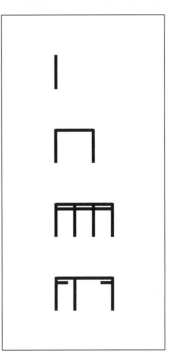

Our new element is also a *syn-co-pa* but is tapped out quickly in the space of one beat. It is made up of a sixteenth, followed by an eighth, followed by a sixteenth. Study the note value relationships shown at the right.

LISTENING

 PLAY CD TRACK 69

Example A

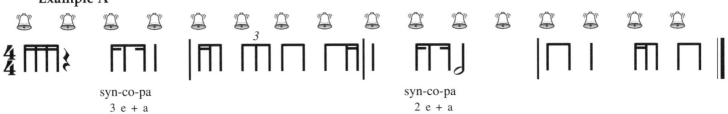

 PLAY CD TRACK 70

The *syn-co-pa* appears in Debussy's delightful "Golliwog's Cakewalk."

TAPPING

For each of the following exercises, tap the rhythm pattern with one hand and the basic beat with the opposite hand.

1.

2.

3.

4.

5.

MATCHING

Match the rhythm boxes shown below with the corresponding exercises on the CD. Mark your answers in the spaces provided. Each exercise consists of more than one rhythm box and is played once on the CD. Answers are on page 47.

PLAY CD TRACK 71

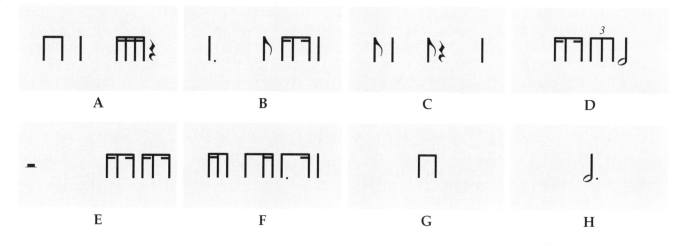

1. _____ 2. _____ 3. _____ 4. _____

37

A	B	C	D

E	F	G	H

5. _____ 6. _____ 7. _____ 8. _____

DICTATION

Play the tracks one at a time. Write the rhythm pattern that you hear. Answers are on page 47.

 PLAY CD TRACK 73–76

1. $\frac{3}{4}$

2. $\frac{4}{4}$

3. $\frac{3}{4}$

4. $\frac{2}{2}$

INTEGRATION

Play the tracks one at a time. Write the melody that you hear.
Answers are on page 47.

PLAY CD TRACK 77–80

1.

s

2.

d

3.

l

4.

d

REVIEW TEST

REVIEW QUESTIONS

1   1. The pick-up bar (a) and the last bar (b) of an exercise are given below. What would the time signature be? _____

a) ♫♫| b) ||♩. ♪||

3   2. Write the traditional counting for the following symbols.

♪ | 　 ♪ 　 ♪ |. 　 ♫♩

_____　　_____　　_____

2   3. a) Write the symbol for the short *syn-co-pa.* _____

b) How many beats would this symbol receive in ⁴⁄₄ time? _____

2   4. a) What is the rhythm name for this symbol? ♪ |. _____

b) How may beats would this grouping receive in ⁴⁄₄ time? _____

1   5. Modify the following symbol so that it could be used in ⁴⁄₄ time. ♫♩

4   6. Find the mistakes in the following exercise and correct them using the blank measures below.

$\frac{3}{4}$ ♫ |♫ ⅞ ♩♫♫ ♪⅞ |. | – |♩.♫ | ⅞ ||

$\frac{3}{4}$ | 　 | 　 | 　 | 　 ||

1   7. Write an alternative symbol for this time signature: ²⁄₂ _____

4   8. Find the mistakes in the following exercise and correct them using the blank measures below.

$\frac{6}{8}$ |. 　 ♪ ♫♩ ⅞ ♩♫♪| ♪ ♫♫|♩. ||

$\frac{6}{8}$ 　 | 　 | 　 | 　 ||

5   9. What is the time value of the following note or group of notes in ⁴⁄₄ time:

♩. ⌣ | 　 o 　 ♪⅞ |. ♪ ♫♫

_____　　_____　_____　_____

40

10. Name the following symbols and fill in the number of beats they would receive in the indicated time signatures. Place an X if the note or rest would not stand alone as a complete element in the given time signature.

Symbol	Rhythm Name	Beats in $\frac{3}{4}$	Beats in $\frac{6}{8}$	Beats in $\frac{4}{4}$
♪ | ♪				
♪ |.				
♫.				
³ ⊓⊓				
ξ.				
⌐ ⌐				
▬				

Each answer is worth one point, for a total of 51 points. Answers are on page 48.
If your score is 47 or better, proceed with the dictations.

YOUR SCORE: _____

Review any areas of weakness before proceeding with the dictations.

DICTATION

PLAY CD TRACK 81–88

POINTS

13   1. $\frac{4}{4}$

12   2. $\frac{3}{4}$

13   3. $\frac{4}{4}$

8   4. $\frac{6}{8}$

13   5. $\frac{4}{4}$

8   6. $\frac{6}{8}$

14   7. **C**

13   8. **¢**

Each note or note grouping is worth one point, for a total of 90 points. Answers are on page 48.
If your score is less than 86, review your areas of weakness and then try the test again.

YOUR SCORE: _____

INTEGRATION

 PLAY CD TRACK 89–94

POINTS

8   1.

d

8   2.

d

14   3.

s

13   4.

s

13   5.

d

13   6.

s

YOUR SCORE:_____

Each correctly-placed note or note grouping is worth one point, for a total of 43 points.
Answers are on page 48. If your score is 39 or more, congratulations, you may proceed to

RHYTHM WITHOUT THE BLUES – VOLUME 4

If you score was less than 39, review your areas of weakness and then try the test again.

ANSWERS

CHAPTER 1

MATCHING:

1. A, C, G, B	2. D, F, A, E, H	3. H, G, C, B, D	4. C, A, E, G
5. C, E, A, G	6. H, F, E, B, D	7. H, C, A, E, D	8. B, G, F, A

DICTATION:

INTEGRATION:

CHAPTER 2

MATCHING:

1. A, E, D, C	2. F, D, A, E, G	3. B, C, E, A	4. F, E, D, B, G
5. B, C, D, A	6. G, B, D, F, H	7. C, F, E, A	8. F, A, D, B

DICTATION:

INTEGRATION:

CHAPTER 3

MATCHING:

1. F, E, B, D, G   2. D, A, C, B   3. A, B, E, C   4. F, C, D, C, G
5. G, B, D, E, H   6. E, C, A, D   7. C, D, B, F   8. G, F, D, A, H

DICTATION:

INTEGRATION:

CHAPTER 4

MATCHING:

1. A, F, D, C   2. G, E, B, C, H   3. D, A, C, F   4. G, D, F, B, H
5. G, B, F, E, H   6. E, C, A, B   7. D, F, A, E   8. A, C, B, D

DICTATION:

INTEGRATION:

CHAPTER 5

MATCHING:

1. E, B, C, D   2. H, A, F, E, G   3. F, C, B, E   4. A, D, F, B

DICTATION:

1.

2.

3.

4.

INTEGRATION:

1.

2.

CHAPTER 6

MATCHING:

1. A, D, F, B   2. C, E, F, A   3. H, C, B, D, G   4. F, A, D, B

5. C, F, E, A   6. H, D, F, B, G   7. F, C, E, B   8. D, A, B, C

DICTATION:

1.

2.

3.

4.

INTEGRATION:

1.

2.

CHAPTER 7

MATCHING:

1. D, A, E, C   2. F, B, D, E   3. B, C, A, D   4. H, E, B, A, G

5. G, F, B, C, H   6. A, D, E, C   7. F, B, A, D   8. B, E, A, C

DICTATION:

INTEGRATION:

CHAPTER 8

MATCHING:

1. A, D, F, C   2. B, E, A, D   3. G, F, D, A, H   4. C, F, B, E

5. B, F, A, C   6. G, E, D, A, H   7. D, F, B, F   8. G, B, A, C, H

DICTATION:

INTEGRATION:

REVIEW TEST

REVIEW QUESTIONS

1. $\frac{3}{4}$

2. (rhythm notation)   1 + 2 +   1 + 2 +   1 + a

3. a) (rhythm)   b) one

4. a) ti-am   b) two

5. (triola rhythm)

6. $\frac{3}{4}$ (rhythm notation)

7. ¢

8. $\frac{6}{8}$ (rhythm notation)

9. four/four/one/two/one

10.

Symbol	Rhythm Name	Beats in $\frac{3}{4}$	Beats in $\frac{6}{8}$	Beats in $\frac{4}{4}$
(symbol)	syn-co-pa	two	x	two
(symbol)	ti-tam	two	x	two
(symbol)	ti-kam	one	x	one
(symbol)	tri-o-la	one	x	one
(symbol)	hush	x	one	x
(symbol)	tim-ka	one	x	one
(symbol)	re-e-e-est	three	two (6 subdivided)	four

DICTATIONS:

1. $\frac{4}{4}$ (rhythm notation)

2. $\frac{3}{4}$ (rhythm notation)

3. $\frac{4}{4}$ (rhythm notation)

4. $\frac{6}{8}$ (rhythm notation)

5. $\frac{4}{4}$ (rhythm notation)

6. $\frac{6}{8}$ (rhythm notation)

7. ¢ (rhythm notation)

8. ¢ (rhythm notation)

INTEGRATION:

1. (musical notation in $\frac{3}{4}$)

2. (musical notation in ¢)

3. (musical notation in $\frac{9}{8}$)

4. (musical notation in $\frac{6}{8}$)

5. (musical notation in ¢)

6. (musical notation in $\frac{3}{4}$)